Let's Classify Animals!

by Kelli Hicks

Science Content Editor:
Kristi Lew

www.rourkepublishing.com

Science content editor: Kristi Lew
A former high school teacher with a background in biochemistry and more than 10 years of experience in cytogenetic laboratories, Kristi Lew specializes in taking complex scientific information and making it fun and interesting for scientists and non-scientists alike. She is the author of more than 20 science books for children and teachers.

www.rourkepublishing.com

Photo credits: Cover © L.Watcharapol , Khramtsova Tatyana, neelsky, Audrey Snider-Bell, pzAxe, Cover logo frog © Eric Pohl, test tube © Sergey Lazarev;; Table of Contents © cristi180884; Page 4 © thumb; Page 5 © sailorr; Page 6 © Andrey Armyagov, Lipowski Milan, ILYA AKINSHIN, Kirsanov; Page 7 © Kirsanov, serg_dibrova; Page 8 © Four Oaks, Uryadnikov Sergey, Monkey Business Images; Page 9 © gary yim; Page 10 © Sari ONeal, Don Fink; Page 11 © Kirsanov; Page 12 © Zadiraka Evgenii, PerseoMedusa; Page 13 © Dr. Morley Read; Page 14 © cristi180884, Johan Larson, Tootles; Page 15 © karamysh; Page 16 © Pinosub, cbpix; Page 17 © Vittorio Bruno; Page 18 © Kokhanchikov, Sabine Schmidt; Page 19 © Czesznak Zsolt; Page 20 © Alekcey, Yongsan; Page 21 © iliuta goean, formiktopus

Editor: Jeanne Sturm

Cover and page design by Nicola Stratford, bdpublishing.com

Library of Congress Cataloging-in-Publication Data

Hicks, Kelli L.
 Let's classify animals! / Kelli Hicks.
     p. cm. -- (My science library)
 Includes bibliographical references and index.
 ISBN 978-1-61741-755-9 (Hard cover) (alk. paper)
 ISBN 978-1-61741-957-7 (Soft cover)
 1. Animals--Classification--Juvenile literature. I. Title.
 QL351.H53 2011
 590--dc22
                            2011004842

Rourke Publishing
Printed in the United States of America,
North Mankato, Minnesota
060711
060711CL

www.rourkepublishing.com - rourke@rourkepublishing.com
Post Office Box 643328 Vero Beach, Florida 32964

Table of Contents

Sorting Species

Did you know there are millions of different kinds of animals, or **species**, living on the Earth? Scientists study these species and classify, or sort, them into groups.

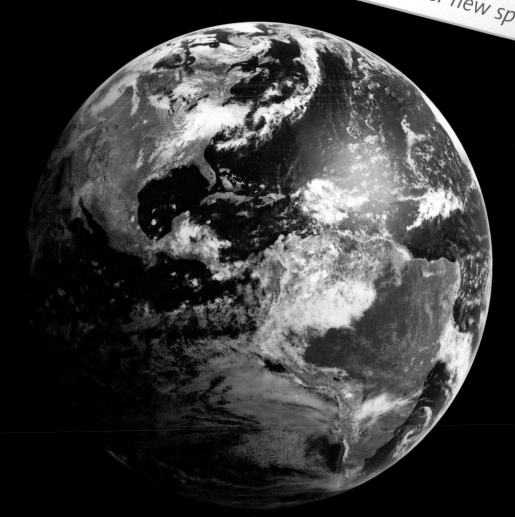

All over the world scientists search the land and sea in order to discover new species.

grasshopper

To classify different species into groups, scientists study what makes species similar and what makes them different. Let's take a closer look.

tarantula

polar bear

Classifying Animals

All the animals that have hair or fur on their bodies are in the same group. They are **warm-blooded** animals and give live birth to their young. The babies drink milk from their mothers. How do we classify these critters?

baby goat

pit viper

They are mammals. Elephants, polar bears, and goats are all mammals. People are mammals too.

Mammals	
Warm-blooded	✔
Give birth to live young	✔
Babies drink milk from mother	✔

African elephants

polar bear with cubs

There is another group of warm-blooded animals. The critters in this group have feathers and wings instead of hair or fur. Their babies **hatch** from eggs. How do we classify these critters?

gentoo penguin with chick

They are birds. Hummingbirds, cardinals, and penguins are all birds. They live in different parts of the world, but they all belong to the same group.

Birds	
Warm-blooded	✔
Babies hatch from eggs	✔
Have feathers and wings	✔

red cardinal

hummingbird

Some critters have **scales** instead of fur or feathers. They are **cold-blooded** animals and have dry skin. Most lay eggs. How do we classify these critters?

pit viper

They are reptiles. Crocodiles, **chameleons**, and snakes are reptiles.

Reptiles	
Cold-blooded	✔
Babies hatch from eggs	✔
Have scales	✔

crocodile

chameleon

Some animals live both on land and in water. They are cold-blooded like reptiles, but have moist skin instead of dry skin. They lay eggs and some have webbed feet. How do we classify these critters?

Amazon leaf frog

They are amphibians. Frogs, toads, and salamanders are all amphibians.

Amphibians	
Cold-blooded	✔
Babies hatch from eggs	✔
Live on land and in water	✔

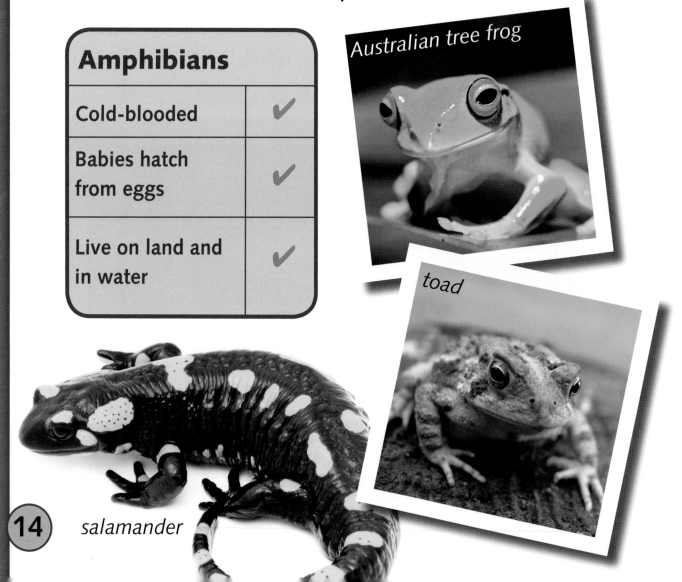

Australian tree frog

toad

salamander

Not all animals breathe above the water. Some breathe underwater with **gills**. They have scales and fins. They are cold-blooded and some lay eggs. How do we classify these critters?

sockeye salmon

They are fish. Did you know that sharks are fish? They belong in the same group with trout, salmon, and guppies.

Fish	
Cold-blooded	✔
Have scales and fins	✔
Breathe underwater with gills	✔

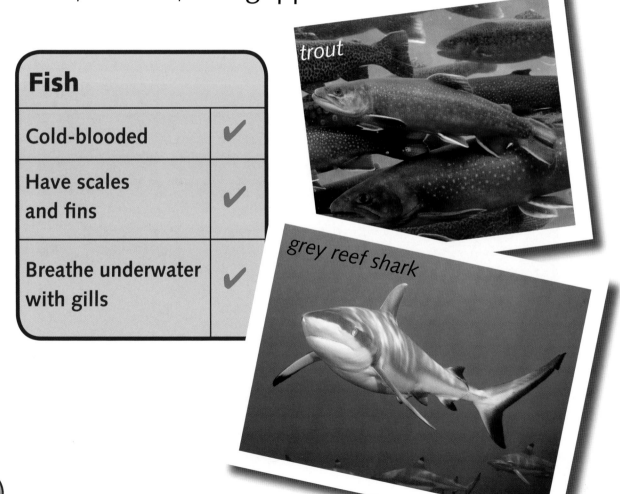

trout

grey reef shark

There is a group of animals that belong together because they don't have a backbone.

octopus

They are invertebrates. Octopuses, earthworms, and snails are all invertebrates.

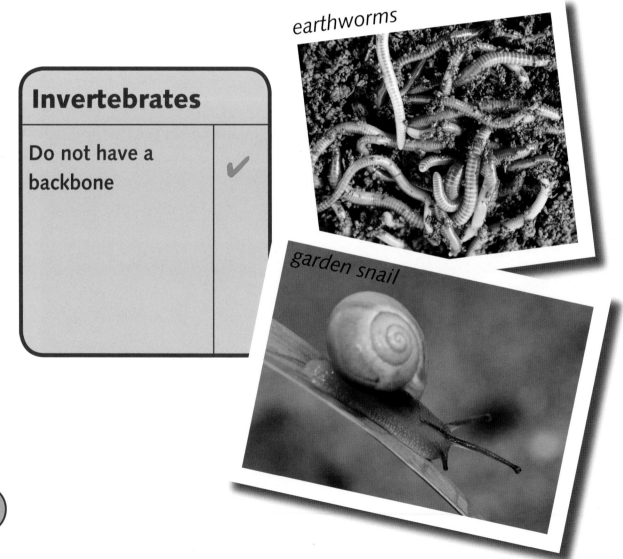

earthworms

garden snail

Invertebrates

Do not have a backbone	✔

Some invertebrates are grouped together because they have multiple body parts and six or more legs. How do we classify these critters?

stag beetle

They are insects and arachnids. Bees, grasshoppers, and beetles are all insects.

Insects	
No backbone	✔
Six legs	✔
Have antennae	✔

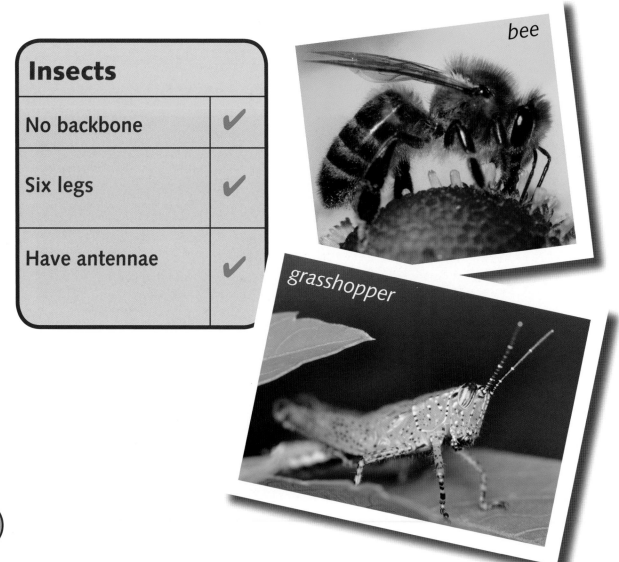

bee

grasshopper

Spiders and scorpions
are arachnids.

scorpion

tarantula

Arachnids	
No backbone	✔
Eight legs	✔
No antennae	✔

SHOW What You Know

1. What are some characteristics of mammals?

2. How would you classify a lizard?

3. Can you explain the similarities and differences between reptiles and amphibians?

Glossary

chameleons (kuh-MEE-lee-uhnz): lizards that can change colors, sometimes matching their surroundings

cold-blooded (KOHLD BLUHD-id): animals whose body temperature changes with the temperature of their surroundings

gills (GILZ): the organs on a fish's side through which it breathes

hatch (HACH): the action of a baby bird or reptile breaking out of its shell

scales (SKALEZ): the small pieces that make the covering on the body of a fish, snake, or other reptile

species (SPEE-sheez): one of the groups of animals sorted according to shared characteristics

warm-blooded (WORM BLUHD-id): animals whose body temperature stays the same even when the temperature of their surroundings changes

Index

Websites

www.brainpopjr.com/science/animals/classifyinganimals/

www.kidsbiology.com

www.kidzone.ws/animals/animal_classes.htm

About the Author

Kelli Hicks would classify herself as a writer, a learner, and someone who loves to curl up in a cozy chair to read a book with her kids. She lives in Tampa with her husband, her kids Mackenzie and Barrett, and their golden retriever Gingerbread.